Updated/Expanded Edition

Cooking with Cicadas

Demonstrate your position at the top of the food chain by
turning cicadas into delicious snacks, meals
and desserts for family and friends

R. Scott Frothingham

Cover Design

(May 2013, using Corel Draw X6, Fonts: Palatino Linotype & Arial)

Cover Photos

Mariano Szklanny (June 19, 2007 using a Canon Powershot A540)

Tim Lindenbaum (May 28, 2007 using a Nikon D80)

Benjamin Gray (May 28, 2007 using a Canon PowerShot A410)

Interior

(May 14, 2013, Microsoft Word97-2003, Fonts: Georgia & Corbel)

Legal Notice: The author and publisher of this recipe book are not entomologists and we are not medical doctors. We have no idea whether or not eating cicadas is safe or potentially harmful. As such, we recommend that you consult a competent expert before consuming cicadas or any other insect (or any food with which you are unfamiliar). We make no representation or warranties with respect to the accuracy, applicability, fitness, or completeness of the contents of this book. The information contained in this book is strictly for entertainment purposes. Therefore, if you wish to apply ideas contained in this book, you are taking full responsibility for your actions.

The author and publisher disclaim any warranties (express or implied), merchantability, or fitness for any particular purpose. The author and publisher shall in no event be held liable to any party for any direct, indirect, punitive, special, incidental or other consequential damages arising directly or indirectly from any use of this material, which is provided "as is", and without warranties.

Dedication

To my fellow dads who do the cooking for their families.
Kevin, Mark, Roy and the rest of you (you know who you are)
and to our families who put up with our adventurous
(and sometimes disastrous) forays into
gastronomic experimentation.

TABLE OF CONTENTS

TABLE OF CONTENTS

Publisher's Preface

This little cookbook is a salute to the adventurous risk-takers of the world who are able to overcome their initial fears and step into areas unknown.

I imagine a few of our ancient ancestors seeing a lobster for the first time. While the group thought, "That's a strange looking creature," and "Those pincers look dangerous" and "Wow, that thing is armor-plated", one brave person stepped forward and said, "Let's eat it for lunch!"

Every time I dig into a steamed lobster and relish in the sweet taste of the delicious meat, I owe a debt of gratitude to that individual who cast off his apprehension and pushed his cultural boundaries in the name of fine dining.

Many people view insects – in this case, the cicada – the same was as our forbearers saw that first lobster. Most will step back in revulsion; some will overcome their trepidation and prepare a meal. This book is here to take that adventurous gourmand to the next level ... from eating a bug to preparing a delicious meal featuring that bug.

And, apparently, there are a lot of culinary explorers out there who are ready to push their boundaries and add periodical cicadas to the menu. Starting almost immediately after this cookbook was published; I was contacted with a wave of feedback including suggested ways of preparing cicadas.

Thus this updated and expanded edition that more than doubles the number of recipes in the original book and includes recipes submitted from outside sources, like *Crispy Wok-Tossed Cicadas* from Andrew Zimmern, the host of the Travel Channel's "Bizarre Foods"; *Sweet Cicada Shish-Kabobs* from Zack Lemann manager of animal and visitor programs at the Audubon Butterfly Garden and Insectarium; *Cicada and Saffron Risotto* from Chris Dovi, Contributing Editor at Richmond Magazine; and *Cicambalaya (Cicada Jambalaya)* from Daniella Martin of GirlMeetsBug.com.

If you would like to submit a recipe for possible inclusion in a future edition of "Cooking with Cicadas", send it in traditional recipe format (list of ingredients followed preparation instructions) and include your name , city and state (and organization, if appropriate) for attribution to CicadaRecipes@FastForwardPublishing.com.

I hope you enjoy the recipes and your adventure into the world of cicada cuisine.

R. Scott Frothingham
Vienna, VA

Introduction

Cicadas.

They're coming whether you like it or not.

What are you going to do?

We suggest eating these crunchy treats that many describe as having a nutty, almond-like flavor.

Entomophagy is defined by the Merriam-Webster Dictionary as "the practice of eating insects." Although the word Entomophagy is relatively new (1975), people have been consuming insects (including ants, crickets, beetles, etc.) for thousands of years.

Perhaps the idea of eating insects does not appeal to you ... maybe we can help when it comes to cicadas. First, we will provide recipes to make them delicious. Second, we will reposition the cicada for you with the following critical information:

> The cicada is an arthropod. You eat other arthropods like lobsters, shrimp and crawfish. So, think of the cicada as a *"land lobster"*.

By the way, many experts agree that cicadas are a rich source of protein (with about the same amount of protein per pound as red meat) and are said to be full of vitamins and minerals, low in fat, and contain virtually zero carbs.

The Arrival of the Cicada.

Millions (billions?) of Cicadas that burrowed underground years ago (13 or 17 years, depending on the brood), will emerge from their subterranean world and start their mating ritual which includes buzzing up to 90 decibels (equivalent to some power motors).

In clusters of up to 1.5 million per acre, it's an incredible natural phenomenon, and it only occurs on the East Coast of the United States (from Connecticut to North Carolina).

There are a variety of ways to view this unique occurrence. Some folks will study it. Some will treat it as a scene from a horror movie. We prefer to view it as a gastronomic opportunity.

A Word About Safety.

We are not experts, and if you have any questions about whether or not to consume cicadas, consult with a competent expert; here is some information we found on the Internet:

1. A number of sources warn that you should not eat cicadas if you are allergic to shellfish. Many sources suggest that since shrimp, lobster, crawfish and cicadas are all arthropods, if you have an allergic reaction to shrimp, lobster and crawfish, you could have an allergic reaction to cicadas.

2. Some sources indicate that scientists warn that cicadas can accumulate a lot of mercury in their lifetime and that should be considered prior to consumption.

3. Many sources suggested that legs, wings and head should be removed before eating and prior to cooking because they are sharp and potential choking hazards.

4. There were a couple of sources that suggested that you consider not eating cicadas that emerge in areas where there has been heavy pesticide use.

5. There are a number of recommendations to flash boil (or blanch) the insects before preparing them. The cicadas themselves are not known to conduct disease but blanching will kill off any soil bacteria on them (and it will firm up the meat). To blanch, drop the cicadas into boiling water for about 5 minutes. After blanching the cicadas can be used in recipes or frozen. NOTE: suggest performing Step 3 above *after* blanching.

Harvesting Cicadas

Before we get to the recipes, here are a couple of tips for you cicada foraging expeditions:

Cicadas are typically not aggressive and their only natural defence is their numbers. They don't bite, sting or pinch, and that makes these inch-long insects easy prey for collection.

1. The best time to catch cicadas is when the temperatures are cooler; e.g., early in the day when they are still sluggish and haven't yet climbed into the trees

2. Freshly hatched (or newly emerged) cicadas (milky white) are considered the best, because their exoskeletons have not yet hardened

3. For the most "meat" (and thus a better meal or snack), select female cicadas (females have pointy abdomens)

Once harvested, if you have no immediate plans for preparation, they freeze well.

OK, let's get to the recipes and some tasty ways to take advantage of the approximately 5-week availability of this high-protein, low fat, gluten free and delicious opportunity.

Starting Simple

Before we tackle the more involved recipes in this book, here are a couple of simple cooking methods that will allow you to taste the cicada in a more pure form.

After these simple dishes, we have provided a selection of international tastes for the cicadas you harvest ... from Italian to Moroccan and Asian to Mexican. We even have ½ dozen dessert recipes for you.

> **Sautéed:** Melt a couple of tablespoons of butter in a small sauté pan and add a couple dozen blanched cicadas. Add the juice of ½ lemon. Sauté until they are slightly brown and crisp. Serve.

> **Dry Roasted:** Pre-heat oven to 225°F. Arrange a couple dozen blanched cicadas on a cookie sheet in a single layer; salt and pepper to taste; place oven for 10-15 minutes (until the meat is dry to the touch). Serve.

NOTE: many choose to cook their cicadas alive; if that is not your preference, one accepted method of euthanasia is putting the cicadas into a plastic bag and then placing that bag into the freezer until the cicadas expire.

Now, let's go gourmet!

Cicada Frittata

Serves 4 to 6

Ingredients:

1 tablespoon butter

2 tablespoons olive oil

½ large red or green pepper, diced

½ medium yellow onion, chopped

1 pound potatoes, shredded (hash browns)

8 eggs, whisked

½ cup blanched cicadas, diced

1 tablespoon water

¾ cup cheddar cheese, shredded

Salt and pepper to taste

Paprika

Instructions:

Preheat oven to 325°F.

Melt butter in an oven-safe frying pan over medium heat. Stir in olive oil and onion, and cook until the onion is translucent (about 10 minutes).

Stir in the potatoes, salt and pepper to taste and continue cooking about 10 minutes (occasionally stirring and flipping).

In a medium bowl, whisk together eggs and water. Add red pepper and cicadas to frying pan, mix in. Pour eggs into the skillet, and reduce heat to low. Sprinkle cheese evenly on top. Cover, and cook 5 minutes.

Cicada Frittata – continued

Transfer the uncovered frying pan to the preheated oven. Bake 10 to 15 minutes, until eggs are no longer runny.
Lightly sprinkle with paprika (as garnish), cut into 8 pieces and serve.

Pasta a la Cicada

Serves 4

Ingredients:

½ pound dry linguine
24 blanched cicadas
2 tablespoons of butter
1 tablespoon of extra virgin olive oil
two cloves of garlic, minced
cup of fresh basil leaves

Instructions:

Boil linguine per instructions on package (al dente). Melt butter in a small sauté pan on medium heat. Add olive oil, garlic, basil and cicadas and sauté until the cicadas are slightly brown and crisp (and the basil wilts). Serve over pasta.

Crispy Wok-Tossed Cicadas

courtesy of Andrew Zimmern, AndrewZimmern.com

Ingredients:

2 cups cicadas

2 tablespoons peanut oil

2 tablespoons minced ginger

1 hot dried Asian chile

4 tablespoons minced lemongrass

1 cup chopped scallions

1 clove minced garlic

2 tablespoons sugar

2 tablespoons Toban Djan (fermented bean paste with chiles)

1 cup minced celery

2 tablespoons soy sauce

1 teaspoon corn starch

3 tablespoons rice wine (or sake)

Instructions:

Collect roughly 2 cups of cicadas, keep them in a bucket (with a lid) with an inch of water inside. Wet wings means they won't fly off! Dry on a towel, pluck wings and legs, and set aside.

Preheat a large wok over high heat. Add the peanut oil, and swirl.

Add the minced ginger, hot dried Asian chile (tsin-tsin work great), minced lemongrass, chopped scallions, minced garlic, sugar, Toban Djan (Lee Kum Kee brand is fine) and toss for 15 seconds. Add the cicadas.

Crispy Wok-Tossed Cicadas – continued

If you can't find fermented bean paste, use a few tablespoons of Chinese dried salted black beans instead.

Toss for one minute to cook. Add the minced celery, toss. Mix the soy sauce, corn starch and rice wine together in a separate bowl, then add the mixture to the wok. Toss, cooking for another minute or so until sauce tightens. Enjoy.

Fried Soft-Shelled Cicadas
Serves 4

courtesy of CDKitchen.com

Ingredients:
> 60 freshly emerged 17 year cicadas
> 3 cups flour
> Salt and pepper to season flour
> 4 eggs, beaten
> 1 cup Corn oil or slightly salted Butter

Instructions:

The best way to prepare them is to dip them, still alive, in beaten egg, roll them in the seasoned flour and then gently sauté them until they are golden brown.

Cicada Fried Rice

Serves 4 to 6

Ingredients:

4 cups cold cooked brown rice
1 ½ cups dry roasted cicadas (see page 11)
1 cup finely chopped scallions
½ cup cooked corn kernels
2 large eggs
1 teaspoon salt (we prefer Kosher salt)
½ teaspoon garlic powder
½ teaspoon powdered ginger
1/8 teaspoon powdered coriander
1 teaspoon fresh coarsely ground black pepper
4 tablespoons oil for stir-frying, or as needed
1 tablespoon soy sauce (we prefer light soy sauce)
½ tablespoon oyster sauce

Instructions:

Lightly beat the eggs with salt, ginger, garlic powder, coriander and pepper.

Heat a large frying pan (or wok) and add 2 tablespoons oil. When the oil is hot, add the eggs. Cook, stirring, until they are lightly scrambled (but not too dry). Put eggs in bowl and wipe the frying pan (or wok) clean. Add 2 tablespoons of oil. Add cooked rice. Stir-fry for a few minutes to break it apart (as wooden spoon works well). Add cicadas and scallions. Stir in soy sauce and oyster sauce as desired. Continue stirring.

When the rice is heated through, add the scrambled egg back into the pan and mix thoroughly. Stir in corn kernels. Serve hot.

Cicada & Summer Vegetable Ragù

courtesy of Mark Terrenzi, Potomac, MD

Ingredients:

4 tablespoons extra virgin olive oil, divided
3-5 cloves garlic, sliced
2 dozen blanched cicadas
2 medium zucchini, sliced ½ inch thick on bias
1 medium to large sweet onion, French cut (Vidalia if available)
1 large sweet bell pepper, seeded and julienned (any color but orange makes a good visual contrast)
25-30 small cherry, grape or pear tomatoes, assorted colors if possible
1 8ounce can tomato sauce
¼-½ cup water, more or less as needed
15 large basil leaves, chopped
2 teaspoons chopped fresh thyme plus extra sprigs for garnish
Salt & pepper

Instructions:

Heat a nonstick pan on medium-high. Sauté cicadas in 1 tablespoon olive oil for 2 minutes, tossing often. Season with salt and pepper while cooking. Remove cicadas from pan and set aside on plate. Wipe pan clean.
Sauté zucchini slices in 1 tablespoon olive oil for 1-2 minutes per side until lightly brown and partially cooked. Season each side with salt and pepper while cooking.

Cicada & Summer Vegetable Ragù – continued

Remove from pan and set aside on plate in a single layer so the slices cool and do not continue to cook. Take care not to overcook the zucchini in this step or it will be mushy in the finished dish. Wipe pan clean. Still on medium-high, heat remaining 2 tablespoons olive oil and add onion and bell pepper. Sauté for 3-4 minutes until beginning to soften. It's OK if the onion and pepper brown slightly but if they are getting very brown, lower heat to medium.

Add garlic slices and season with salt and pepper. Sauté 2 more minutes. Add tomato sauce, ¼ cup water, basil and thyme. Simmer on medium heat for 5-7 minutes until reduced slightly and onions and peppers are tender. Add a bit more water if needed. Add tomatoes and simmer for 3 more minutes.

Add cicadas and zucchini back to pan and incorporate with a spoon. Cover and simmer 2 minutes until everything is heated through. Taste and season with more salt and pepper if necessary. Remove from heat. Garnish with a drizzle of olive oil, a sprinkle of whole fresh thyme leaves stripped from a few sprigs and a few whole sprigs on top. You can also garnish with a pinch of crushed red pepper and/or some grated parmesan or crumbled goat cheese.

Serve in a shallow bowl with crusty bread or with pasta of your choice.

Deep Fried Cicadas

Serves 4 to 6

Ingredients:

Peanut oil (enough to submerge cicadas in pot you are using)

2 dozen blanched cicadas

1 egg

1 tablespoon milk

1 cup all purpose flour

1 teaspoon salt

1 teaspoon pepper

½ teaspoon paprika (prefer hot Hungarian)

½ teaspoon garlic powder

Instructions:

Preheat enough peanut oil to fully submerge the cicadas to about 360°F.

Combine salt, pepper, paprika, garlic powder, and flour in a small bowl.

Combine an egg and a tablespoon of milk in a separate bowl.

Dip the blanched cicadas in the egg wash, then coat them in the flour mix and put into oil to fry for two minutes.

Cicada and Monkfish Sausage

Serves 6

courtesy of Will Wienckowski, Head Chef,
Ipanema Cafe, Richmond, VA

Ingredients:

30 – 50 cicadas, blanched
1 pound monkfish, cut into small pieces (can be replaced with any firm, mild tasting white fish, like Tilapia. Shrimp could be used too)
1 egg white
1-1/2 cup heavy cream
2 tsp. Salt
¼ tsp. White pepper
2 Tbsp. Chopped basil

Instructions:

Arrange the cicadas on a parchment-lined baking sheet, and place into a 350° oven for about 10 minutes, or until the cicadas are dried and crispy. Time will vary depending on the size of the cicadas.

In a food processor, puree the egg white and fish together. Slowly add the heavy cream into the fish and egg mixture as the food processor is running, followed by the salt, white pepper, and basil. Test the seasoning of your sausage by cooking a small spoonful in a non-stick pan, then adjust if necessary.

Carefully pull or snip the wings off of the dry-roasted cicadas. Turn the fish mixture out into a mixing bowl and very gently fold the cicadas in with a rubber spatula. Place the bowl in the refrigerator while you bring a large pot of water to 170°.

Cicada and Monkfish Sausage – continued

To shape the links, place two to three ounces of sausage mix near the bottom edge of a square of plastic wrap. Roll the sausage up tightly from the bottom, shaping the link as you go.

Twist both open ends up to seal the link. Repeat this for the rest of the sausage mix, then poach the sausages in the 170° water until the internal temperature of the sausages is at least 140°. Remove the sausages from the pot and place into a bowl of ice water to stop the cooking process. Once chilled, the sausages can be unwrapped, carefully removed from the water and patted dry with a paper towel.

Place a large heavy skillet over medium heat. Once hot, coat the pan with oil and begin to cook the sausages in batches that will not crowd the pan. Allow the sausages to get golden brown on one side, then gently turn the sausages to brown on the other side. Serve immediately, or place in a warm (no more than 200°) oven until serving time.

Bacon Cicadas

Courtesy of Pete Reader, West Orange, NJ

Ingredients:

½ pound bacon

1 medium yellow onion

¼ teaspoon of salt

½ teaspoon ground rosemary

¼ teaspoon ground pepper

1 dozen fresh cicadas (just pull them off the trees.)

Instructions:

Cut bacon strips into small squares and place in a medium skillet (10"). Turn on and heat on a medium heat. As the bacon begins to render, slice the medium onion into thin slices and stir into the bacon. When the onions have softened in the pan, add salt and pepper. As the bacon begins to brown, add the cicadas and stir. The cicadas and bacon will begin to brown. Add to the rosemary and stir. When the cicadas and the bacon have reached a nice light brown color, turn off the heat and plate. The cicadas and bacon should have a nice flavorful crunch that can be added to salads or just a side dish with rice.

Cicada Tostadas
Serves 4

Ingredients:

  1/2 pound dry roasted cicadas (see page 11)
  2 cloves garlic, minced
  1 lemon
  Salt
  2 ripe avocados, mashed
  Canola oil
  6 corn tortillas

Instructions:

Pour ¼ inch layer of oil into a frying pan. Heat the oil on medium high heat until sizzling hot (but not smoking). One at a time, fry the tortillas in the oil. Bubbles should form in the tortilla immediately as you put the tortilla in the oil (otherwise the oil is not hot enough). Fry until golden brown on both sides (about 30 to 60 seconds per side). Use metal tongs or a spatula to push the tortilla down in the oil, and to turn and lift the tortilla out of the pan, draining the excess oil as you do so. The tortilla should be fairly stiff and crisp (if not, the oil is not hot enough.) Place the fried tortilla on a paper towel-lined plate, to absorb the excess oil. Sprinkle with a little salt.
Put the cooked tortillas on a rimmed baking sheet and place in a 250°F oven to keep warm. Add more oil to the pan as needed; make sure the oil heats sufficiently before adding a tortilla.

Cicada Tostadas – continued

Toss cicadas with garlic, juice from 1 lemon, and salt to taste. Spread mashed avocado on the fried tortillas. Sprinkle on cicadas.

Quick Cicada Quiche
Serves 6

Ingredients:

1/2 cup onion, chopped
18 blanched cicadas
5 ounces Swiss cheese, shredded
3 ounces Parmesan cheese, grated
1 frozen 9 inch deep dish pie crust
4 eggs, lightly beaten
1 cup "half-and-half" (½ cream, ½ milk)

Instructions:

Preheat oven to 400°F.
In a medium bowl, mix the cicadas, onions, and both cheeses. Place this mixture in the unthawed pie crust. Mix the eggs and half and half in a bowl. Pour the egg mixture over the cheese mixture.
Bake in preheated oven for 15 minutes. Reduce heat to 350°F and bake for an additional 35 minutes, until top of quiche begins to turn brown.
Serve.

Cicada and Saffron Risotto

Serves 4

courtesy of Chris Dovi, Contributing Editor at Richmond Magazine

Ingredients:

1 medium onion, diced
4 stalks of celery, diced
2 tablespoons of olive oil
2 1/2 cups of chicken stock
12 to 15 cicadas, wings plucked
1 cup of Arborio rice
1/2 cup Parmesan cheese
4 to 5 strands of saffron

Instructions:

In a medium pot, heat 1 tablespoon of the olive oil and add the onions and celery. Sauté until soft. Add the Arborio rice. Coat in the olive oil and lightly toast the rice. Do not brown. Add chicken stock to cover, reduce the heat to medium-low and stir constantly until liquid begins to absorb. Add more stock a little at a time and continue to stir and reduce the mixture until the rice becomes tender. After half of stock is used, add the saffron strands and continue stirring and adding more stock. When the rice is nearly done, add the cicadas. Contemplate life and death as cicadas briefly crawl around in risotto before succumbing to their now-slightly creamy fate. Add any remaining liquid and continue stirring until the liquid is absorbed, and the cicadas appear parboiled. Remove from the heat, and carefully stir in Parmesan cheese. Serve

Cicadas 'n' Greens

Serves 4 to 6

Ingredients:

1 large bunch of spinach (about 12 cups leaves), washed

1 medium bunch of beet greens, washed and chopped

½ cup blanched cicadas

1 ½ tablespoons extra virgin olive oil

2 garlic cloves, finely chopped

2 teaspoons fresh lemon juice

½ teaspoon salt (we prefer Kosher salt)

1 teaspoon freshly ground black pepper

1 tablespoon toasted pine nuts

1 lemon (sliced into wedges)

Instructions:

Heat the oil in a deep frying pan over medium-high heat.

Toss in cicadas and sauté for 3-4 minutes.

Add the garlic and lemon juice and sauté another 2 minutes.

Turn the heat to high and add beet greens and ¼ teaspoon salt; cook for 2-3 minutes.

Add spinach tossing with tongs to coat the leaves with the hot oil, garlic and other ingredients until all ingredients are thoroughly blended and spinach is wilted.

Add pine nuts.

Add salt and pepper to taste.

Serve immediately with lemon wedge.

Cicada Chips

Serves 2 to 4

courtesy of Yellow Kim on Food.com

Ingredients:

    30-40 cicadas
    1 teaspoon salt
    1 teaspoon pepper
    1/2 teaspoon paprika
    1/2 teaspoon garlic powder
    1 cup flour
    1 egg
    1 tablespoon milk
    oil (for frying

Instructions:

    Heat oil in a pan.
    Find the Adult Cicada they are the ones with red eyes
    and clear colored wings. You can either find them by
    following their beautiful screeching sound or just locate
    any tree.
    Leave them as is no need to tear off wings or legs they
    add to the crispyness.
    Mix together flour and seasonings.
    Mix together milk and egg.
    First dip cicada into egg then into flour mixture. Then
    drop into oil. Don't worry they won't try to fly away they
    are too dumb for that.
    Fry them for no longer the 2 minutes.
    Transfer to paper towels. Then serve immediately.
    I like a little hot pepper on mine but you can also use
    ketchup for the kids.

Chili con Cicadas

Serves 6 to 8

Ingredients:

4 slices bacon

1 ½ pounds ground beef

½ pound ground pork

2 cups of blanched cicadas

1 large onion, chopped

1 large green bell pepper, chopped

4 cloves garlic, finely chopped

1/4 cup chili powder

2 tablespoons unsweetened cocoa powder

1 tablespoon ground cumin

2 teaspoons dried oregano

2 teaspoons paprika

1 teaspoon salt (we use Kosher salt)

2 ounces of tomato paste

1 12-ounce bottle beer (we use an amber beer like Brooklyn Lager ... or ... in the spirit of this adventure, use the India Pale Ale called "Infestation" brewed by Mikkeler, a Danish brewer)

2 cans of diced tomatoes (14.5-ounce each)

1 1/2 cups beef broth (we suggest low-sodium), plus more if needed

1 tablespoon hot sauce (we like Frank's Red Hot or Texas Pete)

Shredded cheddar cheese

Instructions:

Cook the bacon in a large saucepan over medium heat until crisp (6 to 8 minutes per side). Drain on a paper towels and let cool; then crumble and set aside.

Chili con Cicadas – continued

Pour off all but 1 tablespoon of the bacon drippings from the saucepan (save the drippings).

Increase the heat to medium-high; add the beef and pork and cook, breaking up the meat with a wooden spoon, until browned (about 8 minutes). Transfer to a plate using a slotted spoon; discard fat left in the pan and wipe it with a paper towel.

Over medium-high heat, heat 1 tablespoon of the reserved bacon drippings in the saucepan. Add the onion and bell pepper and cook, stirring, until soft (about 5 minutes). Add the garlic and 1 teaspoon salt and cook 2 minutes. Add the chili powder, cumin, paprika, oregano and tomato paste and cook, stirring for 5 minutes (add a splash of water if the mixture begins to stick). Add the beer and simmer until almost completely reduced (about 3 minutes).

Stir in the beef (and any juices from the plate); add the tomatoes, beef broth, cicadas and cocoa powder and bring to a simmer over low heat. Cook, stirring occasionally, until the chili thickens slightly (about 1 ½ hours).

Stir the hot sauce into the chili. If the chili is too thick, add some beef broth.

Serve topped with the crumbled bacon and cheddar cheese.

Charleston Cheese Grits and Blackened Cicadas with Grilled Onions & Peppers

4 to 6 servings

courtesy of Jason Alley, owner and Head Chef, Comfort Restaurant and Pasture Restaurant, Richmond, VA

Ingredients:

30-40 cicadas (gathered as they emerge from the ground, remove heads, legs and wings)
1 red pepper, thinly sliced
1 green pepper, thinly sliced
1 tablespoon olive oil
1 1/2 tablespoons Blackened Seasoning (recipe follows)
Salt and pepper to taste
1 tablespoon butter
Charleston Cheese Grits (recipe follows)

Instructions:

In a small saucepan, bring 2 cups water to boil. Add cicadas and boil 4-5 minutes. Drain and set aside. Grill peppers and onions until al dente, season with salt and pepper. Set aside.
Heat sauté pan until hot. Add olive oil, then cicadas. Sauté 1-2 minutes. Add Blackened Seasoning, onions and peppers. Sauté 1-2 minutes more. Finish with butter.
Serve over Charleston Cheese Grits.

Charleston Cheese Grits and Blackened Cicadas
with Grilled Onions & Peppers – continued

Charleston Cheese Grits

Ingredients:

    1 1/2 cups quick-cooking or old-fashioned grits
    1 teaspoon salt plus more to taste
    2 cups milk
    1 cup heavy cream
    6 tablespoons butter
    Fresh ground black pepper

Instructions:

In large, heavy saucepan, bring 6 cups water to a boil. Add grits and 1 tsp. Salt, stir to combine. When grits thicken, add milk, cream and butter then return to boil. Reduce to simmer, cover and cook 45 minutes to 1 hour, or until grits are tender, smooth and creamy. Season with salt and pepper to taste.

Charleston Cheese Grits and Blackened Cicadas with Grilled Onions & Peppers – continued

Blackened Seasoning

Ingredients:

1 1/2 tablespoons paprika

1 tablespoon garlic powder

1 tablespoon onion powder

1 tablespoon thyme

1 teaspoon ground black pepper

1 teaspoon cayenne pepper

1 teaspoon oregano

1 teaspoon salt

1 teaspoon pepper

Instructions:

Mix ingredients thoroughly.

Shanghai Cicadas
Serves 4 to 6 (appetizer portions)

Cicadas are considered a delicacy in the city of Shanghai in China. This is an adaptation of a traditional recipe

Ingredients:

Peanut oil
2 dozen cicadas
2 tablespoons anise seeds
2 cups rice wine
2 tablespoons soy sauce
10 cloves mashed garlic
turnip greens (for garnish)

Instructions:

Put rice wine, anise seeds and 1 tablespoon of soy sauce into a small pot and bring to boil.
Add cicadas and leave on a gentle boil for 5 minutes.
In a small fry pan, sauté the mashed garlic and the remaining tablespoon of soy sauce to make a thick paste (if you need more liquid add some of the boiling liquid (wine, soy, anise).
Deep-fry the wine boiled cicadas (fully submerged the in 360°F peanut oil), then skewer them with bamboo picks.
Place turnip greens on plate, top with a puddle of garlic paste, place skewered cicadas on the paste.

Jerk Cicadas

courtesy of Mark Wolff, Vienna, VA

Ingredients:

Juice of 2 limes (about 1 ½ cups)
1 tablespoon oil
1 teaspoon molasses
1 teaspoon cinnamon
1 teaspoon thyme
1 teaspoon allspice
1 teaspoon ground ginger
1 teaspoon chopped garlic
1 teaspoon soy sauce
1 teaspoon finely chopped jalapeno pepper
1 scallion chopped
1 shot dark rum (optional – for the marinade or the chef)
3-4 Plantains

Instructions:

Combine all ingredients except plantains, whisk together.Place 1-2 dozen cicadas (thawed, blanched, or fresh) into a bowl with the marinade; mix to thoroughly cover cicadas with marinade. Refrigerate for 1 hour. Next, prepare the plantains; peel and slice diagonally making oval shaped slices.
Heat a skillet with 2 tablespoons peanut oil to medium heat. Place plantain slices in skillet and remove when browned and cooked through. Place plantains on plate with paper towels to drain and keep warm.
Drain some of the oil from the pan, reserving enough to sauté.
Remove the cicadas from the marinade and place the cicadas in the skillet and sauté on medium heat for 2-3 minutes.
Remove from heat and serve with warm plantains.

Cicada Pâté

Ingredients:

    1/3 pound blanched cicadas
    10 chicken livers
    4 cloves garlic
    1 small onion
    1/8 teaspoon salt
    1 tablespoon dry sherry
    Black pepper, to taste
    Oregano, to taste
    Marjoram, to taste
    Olive oil, to taste

Instructions:

Place the chicken livers in a saucepan with the garlic, onion, salt, and enough water to cover. Bring to a boil and simmer for 10 minutes.

Remove the chicken livers and place in a blender or food processor reserving the broth. Add the cicadas, sherry and about 1/4 cup of the reserved broth and purée, adding more broth as needed, until mixture is smooth and reaches a spreadable consistency. Add spices and oil to taste. Place in a wooden bowl and serve with crusty French bread

Double Sautéed Cicada Nymphs

Serves 4

courtesy of M. Eigh,
from his book "The Cicada Survival Guide"

The young cicada nymphs harvested mid-molting offer the most tender texture and deserve a cooking method that best preserves their natural moisture and injects a balanced blend of flavor.

What can better achieve that end than the double sauté method?

Ingredients:

> 1 tablespoon of sake or cooking wine of any type
> 2 tablespoons of canola or other type of vegetable oil
> 6 cloves garlic, finely chopped
> 1 tablespoon minced fresh ginger root.
> 1 thumb-sized fresh ginger root. Flatten it between two cutting boards, or simply smash it flat with a cleaver
> 2 cups large cicada nymphs, wings (if developed) and legs clipped and cleaned
> 1/2 cup soy sauce.
> 1 tablespoon brown sugar
> 1 teaspoon rice vinegar
> 1 tablespoon Chinese miso or Japanese miso paste. For people who can handle spice, use Chinese Toban Djan, a.k.a., Chilli Bean Sauce, instead.
> 2 stalks finely chopped leeks
> Japanese Nichimi Togarashi (seven-flavor spice) to taste

Double Sautéed Cicada Nymphs – continued

Instructions:

Place flattened ginger root in a deep soup pot. Add two quarts of water and bring to a boil. Place cicada nymphs into the boiling water, turn down the fire to low and let the pot simmer for 3 minutes. Drain when done. Caution: Never put any salt in the pot, as salt will dehydrate the nymphs and rob them of their natural moisture.

Heat the vegetable oil in a wok, then add the minced ginger and chopped garlic. Add soy sauce and give the mix a good swirl and stir before you add in the drained nymphs.

Add sake or cooking wine and keep stirring over high heat. Add brown sugar and vinegar and stir. Finally, add miso paste and stir vigorously.

Add chopped leeks and stir for 30 seconds.

Sprinkle Nichimi Togarashi to taste.

Double sautéed nymphs go well with brown or white rice, cuscus, quinoa, nan or roti.

Cicada Chermoula

Serves 2

Ingredients:

    3 ½ tablespoons butter
    3 teaspoons of Canola Oil
    ½ cup of blanched cicadas
    2/3 cup of baby spinach
    1 lime (juiced)
    ¼ cup fresh cilantro, chopped
    1 clove of garlic, minced
    ½ teaspoon paprika
    ¼ teaspoon powdered cumin
    ¼ teaspoon chili powder
    salt

Instructions:

Blend butter, lime, cilantro, garlic, paprika, cumin and chili powder and set aside.

Heat oil in deep frying pan (or wok) over a medium heat. Add cicadas and sauté for 1 to 2 minutes.

Add butter mixture and stir gently until completely melted.

Add spinach and toss until it starts to wilt.

Serve immediately.

Cabo Wabo Cicada Tacos

courtesy of Jason Alley, owner and head chef, Comfort Restaurant and Pasture Restaurant, Richmond, VA

Ingredients:
   3 flour tortillas
   cilantro sprigs for garnish
For the cicadas:
   24 cicadas
   1/2 cup buttermilk
   1 cup all purpose flour
   salt and pepper to taste
   4 cups vegetable oil for frying
For the slaw:
   2 cups shredded cabbage
   1 shallot, peeled and julienned
   1 small jalapeño, seeded and julienned
   juice of one lime
   salt and pepper to taste
   For the mayonnaise:
   1/2 cup Duke's mayonnaise
   1 tablespoon hot sauce of your preference

Instructions:

   Bring a large pot of heavily salted water to a boil.
   Remove the wings from the bugs. Blanch the cicadas in
   the boiling water for 1 minute. Transfer the critters to a
   bowl of ice water to stop the cooking. Drain the cicadas
   and pat dry.
   Heat the oil in a heavy pot to 350 degrees.

Cabo Wabo Cicada Tacos – continued

Soak the bugs in the buttermilk. With a slotted spoon, remove the cicadas from the buttermilk, and dredge in the seasoned flour. Reserve the breaded bugs.
Combine all the ingredients for the slaw, refrigerate until ready to serve.
Combine the mayo and hot sauce, refrigerate until ready to serve.
Fry the critters in batches until just golden, and drain on paper towels.
Serve the cicadas in warm tortillas, garnish with the slaw, spicy mayonnaise, and cilantro. Eat while hot with lots of beer (lots and lots of beer).

Cicada Fritters

Serves 6 to 8

Ingredients:

1 ¾ cups of all-purpose flour
2 tablespoons cornstarch
2 teaspoons baking powder
2 eggs plus 2 egg whites
¼ cup milk
1 pound blanched cicadas, chopped
½ green pepper, finely chopped
½ red pepper, finely chopped
½ yellow pepper, finely chopped
1 red onion, finely chopped
2 stalks of celery, finely chopped
2 cloves of garlic, minced
½ teaspoon salt
pinch of pepper
dash of hot pepper sauce
oil for frying (we use peanut oil)

Instructions:

Sift together flour and cornstarch, baking powder and salt. In a large mixing bowl whip together eggs, egg whites, and milk. Combine flour mixture with liquid ingredients. Add all other ingredients and mix well. Heat a pot deep enough to submerge fritters to 375°F. Form into 1 to 2 inch balls (about 1 ounce). Submerge balls in oil and fry until golden brown (about 3 to 5 minutes) Add Fritters one at a time waiting a few seconds to avoid quickly reducing the oil temperature. Remove from oil and place on paper towel to drain excess oil. Serve with favorite sauce.

Cicada Nachos

Serves 8 (appetizer portions)

Ingredients:

- 1 pound of large tortilla corn chips
- 1 cup of dry-roasted cicadas (see page 11)
- ¼ cup black olives (sliced)
- ¼ cup of fresh jalapeño peppers
- 2 teaspoons fresh chopped cilantro
- 2 cups shredded cheddar cheese
- 1 teaspoons chili powder
- 1 teaspoons olive oil
- Salt

Instructions:

Toss cicadas, olive oil and chili powder and a pinch of salt in a small bowl. Add the olives, jalapeños and cilantro.

On microwavable platter, put layer of chips followed by ¼ of the cicada, olive, jalapeño, cilantro mixture.

Then place a layer of cheese.

Continue these layers until you have used up the cicada, olive, jalapeño, cilantro mixture.

Top with cheese and place into microwave until cheese melts (about 45 seconds).

Cicambalaya (Cicada Jambalaya)

courtesy of Daniella Martin, GirlMeetsBug.com

Ingredients:

1 pound frozen, raw cicadas
½ pound chopped andouille sausage
2 cups chicken broth
1 green bell pepper, chopped
1 onion, chopped
2 ribs celery, chopped
4 garlic cloves, minced
1 14 oz can diced tomatoes
1 cup uncooked long-grain rice
1 tsp Cajun seasoning
4 scallions, chopped
olive oil
salt
pepper
cayenne
fresh thyme
bay leaf

Instructions:

Sauté the sausage in olive oil for 4-5 minutes, until it browns. Add chopped onions, peppers, celery, and a pinch of cayenne; sauté until softened. Add garlic and cook for 2 more minutes. Next, add tomatoes, Cajun seasoning, rice, chicken broth, teaspoon of thyme, and bay leaf. Season with salt to taste, and cook for 25 minutes on medium heat. When rice is cooked (or nearly there), add in cicadas and cook for 5-7 more minutes. Serve garnished with chopped scallions.

Cicada Salad

Serves 4

Ingredients:

 1 bag of mixed spring lettuce, washed
 ½ cup blanched cicadas
 ½ lime, juiced
 ¼ cup extra virgin olive oil
 1 quartered tomato
 ½ sliced red onion
 2 teaspoons capers
 1/3 cup Feta cheese
 Pine nuts
 Dried cranberries
 Salt
 Pepper

Instructions:

Add 1 tablespoon oil, capers, cicadas and a pinch of salt into a frying pan over medium-high and sauté. When the cicadas are heated through, mix in 1 tablespoon of lime juice and them remove from heat and allow to cool.

Place lettuce, tomatoes, and onions in a serving bowl. Add to salad the remaining olive oil and lime juice and toss thoroughly and pepper to taste. Pour cooked cicadas (with pan juices) over the lettuce and garnish with the Feta, pine nuts and dried cranberries.

Cicada Tacos

Serves 4

courtesy of Will Wienckowski, Head Chef at Ipanema Cafe,
Richmond, VA

Ingredients:

30-40 cicadas, blanched
4 roma tomatoes
1 jalapeno pepper
2 cloves of garlic
1/4 cup cilantro, chopped
1 tsp. Ground cumin
1 head of bok choy
1 shallot, sliced thin
1 Tbsp. Olive oil
1 tsp. Lime juice
2 cups cornstarch
2 large eggs
Vegetable oil for frying
white corn tortillas
kosher salt

Instructions:

Over a flame, or in a hot cast iron skillet, char the tomatoes and jalapeno pepper until soft and blackened. Remove the skins and remove the seeds from the pepper. Quarter the tomatoes, and dice the jalapeno. With a mortar and pestle, crush the garlic cloves then add the tomatoes, peppers, cilantro, and cumin. Season to taste with kosher salt.

Wash the bok choy, then cut it into strips. Mix the bok choy, shallot, olive oil, and lime juice together and season with kosher salt.

Cicada Tacos – continued

In a bowl, whisk the two eggs together with 2 Tbsp. of water.

Dust the cicadas with cornstarch, coat with beaten egg, then return them to the cornstarch. Shake off any excess cornstarch, then place the cicadas on a plate or baking rack (The cicadas can be fried whole or with the wings and legs removed).

In a heavy bottomed frying pan, heat enough vegetable oil to almost cover a cicada. Once hot, begin frying the cicadas in batches if necessary. After about 2 minutes frying in hot oil, the cicadas should be cooked and crispy. Scoop them out with a slotted spoon onto paper towels.

Put the bok choy, cicadas, and tomato salsa into warm corn tortillas and serve with any desired garnishes (any garnish can be added to the tacos. I recommend sliced radish, queso fresco, and a little lime juice squeezed on top).

BBQ Cicada Sandwich

Serves 2

Ingredients:

    ½ cup BBQ sauce
    ¼ pound coleslaw
    2 dozen blanched cicadas
    2 hamburger buns or Kaiser rolls

Instructions:

Put the cicadas and the BBQ sauce in a small pan and heat through on medium heat (approximately 10 minutes).

Open the hamburger buns/Kaiser rolls and divide the hot cicada, BBQ sauce mixture evenly between the two buns/rolls.

Put ½ of the coleslaw on top of the cicada/sauce. Put the top of the bun/roll on top of the coleslaw.

Dig in and enjoy.

Cicada Mousseline

Serves 4 (or 24 appetizer portions)

Ingredients:

2 dozen blanched cicadas (legs, heads & wings removed), cut in half
2 pound sole fillets, cut into 1-inch pieces
1 tablespoon + ½ teaspoon Kosher Salt
½ teaspoon white pepper
4 egg whites
1 2/3 cups heavy cream
4 ounces Dijon-style prepared mustard
1 tablespoon + 1 teaspoon fresh chives, diced
2 teaspoons fresh tarragon, chopped
1/8 teaspoon ground nutmeg
Butter
Paprika
White bread, thinly sliced

Instructions:

Preheat oven to 350°F.
Put cicadas, sole, salt and pepper in a chilled food processor bowl and use pulse action to process until smooth. Add egg whites; pulse until blended. Transfer to mixing bowl. Place filled bowl in ice bath; fold in cream, mustard, 1 tablespoon of chives, tarragon and nutmeg. Refrigerate until ready to use.
Butter 6 ramekins (or a terrine) and put a round of parchment paper in the bottom of each. Fill the ramekins with the cicada mixture. Set them in a baking dish and pour boiling water around to come half-way up the sides. Bake until just set, about 20 minutes.

Cicada Mousseline – continued

While cicada mixture is cooking, remove the crust from the bread slices, toast to golden brown and cut into points (or rounds using a cookie cutter.)
Unmold onto warm serving plates (remove parchment), lightly dust with paprika and garnish with chives. Arrange toast next to it/around it to create an appetizing presentation.

Cicada Pad Thai

Serves 6 to 8

Ingredients:

10 oz rice noodles (sticks)
6 tablespoons fish sauce
2 tablespoons soy sauce
6 tablespoons lime juice
4 teaspoons natural sugar (e.g., Turbinado)
4 tablespoons peanut oil
1 cup blanched cicadas
4 cloves garlic
3 eggs – lightly beaten
½ cup scallions, finely chopped
2 cups bean sprouts
¼ cup crushed peanuts
½ cup fresh cilantro
1 lime (cut into wedges)

Instructions:

While cooking rice noodles (about 10 minutes in boiling water), in a separate bowl combine the fish sauce, soy sauce, lime juice and sugar in a bowl and blend well. Pour oil into a frying pan (or wok) on medium-high heat. Add cicadas and eggs and scramble.
Remove cicadas and eggs (set aside in bowl).
Add garlic and scallions to frying pan and fry until soft. Add sauce mixture, cicadas and eggs back into the frying pan and warm thoroughly.
Remove and drain noodles, and add to frying pan. Add in bean sprouts and toss thoroughly (be careful not to break the noodles). Top with peanuts, cilantro, and garnish with a lime wedge.

Grilled Cicadas with Summer Veggies
Serves 4
courtesy of Chris Dovi, Contributing Editor at Richmond Magazine

Ingredients:
15 to 20 fresh cicadas
2 zucchini or summer squash, quartered lengthwise
12 asparagus spears, woody ends snapped off
12 yellow cherry tomatoes
1 tablespoon of olive oil
Salt, to taste

Instructions:

Prepare the vegetables and arrange on a sheet of aluminum foil. Arrange the cicadas on the sheet interspersed among the vegetables. Reconsider McDonalds as a legitimate lunch option as you watch the cicadas crawl slowly among veggies. Drizzle with olive and sprinkle liberally with salt. Cover with a second sheet of aluminum foil and crimp the edges to create a packet. Place on the grill at medium heat and close the grill. Cook approximately 15 minutes or until the vegetables are tender. The cicadas will be dead.

Cicada Etouffée

Serves 6

Ingredients:

1 ½ pounds blanched cicadas

1 tablespoon Cajun or Creole spice (more or less to taste – we like 1 ½ tablespoons)

4 tablespoons butter

3 tablespoons of flour

½ cup diced onions

½ cup celery, sliced thin

½ cup diced green bell pepper

2 cloves garlic, minced

1 tablespoon dried parsley

salt (we like Kosher) and black pepper (fresh ground) to taste

3 cups chicken stock

½ cup diced tomatoes

1 bay leaf

1 teaspoon Worcestershire sauce

½ cup scallions, minced

Hot sauce to taste (we use Frank's or Texas Pete)

8 cups cooked rice (white or brown)

Instructions:

In a medium sized bowl combine the cicadas with the Cajun/Creole seasoning; mix well.

Over medium heat, melt the butter in a heavy bottomed pot and cook over low heat until it foams. Add the flour and cook, stirring, for about 10 minutes to make a roux. The roux should stay golden in color (don't let it get too brown).

Cicada Etouffée – continued

Add the onions, celery, green bell pepper, parsley, salt and pepper; cook in the roux for 5 minutes (until the vegetables start to soften). Whisk in the stock, tomatoes, bay leaf, and Worcestershire sauce; turn the heat up to high and bring to a simmer. Reduce heat to low and simmer uncovered for 25 minutes (until the vegetables are tender and the mixture has thickened). Stir in the cicadas, scallions, and hot sauce; simmer for 5 minutes. Taste to determine whether or not to add more Cajun/Creole seasoning, salt, pepper and/or hot sauce. Serve with hot rice.

Quick Cicada Tacos

Serves 8

Ingredients:

2 tablespoons butter

½ pound blanched cicadas

3 tablespoons taco seasoning mix

3/4 cup water

1 can of black beans

1 can small dice tomatoes w/ basil, garlic and oregano

1 package hard taco shells (soft corn tortillas can be substituted)

2 cups lettuce, shredded

1 cup Cheddar cheese, shredded

sour cream

Instructions:

Heat butter in a frying pan over medium heat.

Add cicadas and sauté for 10 minutes (or until cooked through).

Add water, beans, diced tomatoes and taco seasoning. Simmer until desired consistency.

To serve, spoon mixture into taco shells, top with sour cream, lettuce and cheese.

Soft-Shelled Cicadas

Serves 4
courtesy of Sassafrasnanc (Food.com)

Ingredients:
1 cup Worcestershire sauce
60 freshly emerged 17 year cicadas
4 eggs, beaten
3 cups flour
2 tablespoons salt
2 tablespoons black pepper
1 teaspoon cayenne pepper (optional)
1 cup corn oil or 1 cup salted butter

Instructions:

Marinate cicadas, alive in a sealed container, in Worcestershire sauce for several hours.
Dip them, in beaten egg, roll them in the seasoned flour and then gently sauté them until they are golden brown.

Cicada Curry

Serves 4

Ingredients

Rice (cooked according to package instructions)
2 tbsp vegetable oil (we use canola)
1 can of diced or crushed tomatoes
1 medium red onion, chopped
2 cloves garlic, diced
30 blanched cicadas
3 tablespoons curry powder
1/2 teaspoon cumin powder
1 teaspoon ginger powder
1/4 teaspoon cayenne pepper powder
2 tablespoons fresh cilantro, chopped

Instructions:

Heat the oil in a frying pan (or wok) over high heat.
Add the onion and stir well, reduce heat to medium
high and cook onions until translucent.
Add the garlic and sauté until the garlic turns light
brown.
Add curry powder, cumin, ginger and cayenne. Stir
well. Cook for a minute or two.
Add the tomatoes and stir occasionally (. You want to
the tomatoes' water evaporate, so the sauce is thicker ...
to the consistency of a typical Italian tomato sauce for
pasta.
Add cicadas. Stir well, to let it absorb the ingredients
(about 5 minutes). If the sauce starts gets too dry, mix
in some water.
Serve over rice. Add the cilantro as garnish.

Kung Pow Cicadas

courtesy of Jason Alley, owner and head chef, Comfort Restaurant
and Pasture Restaurant, Richmond, VA

Ingredients:

15-20 cicadas, wings removed
2 stalks celery, diced
1 large shallot, peeled and diced
3 scallions, root trimmed, and sliced
2 cloves garlic, minced
1 Tbs. Ginger, minced
1/2 cup roasted, salted peanuts
2 Tbs. Oyster sauce
1 tsp. Tamari
1 tsp. Sambal paste
1 Tbs. vegetable oil for sautéing

Instructions:

Bring a large pot of heavily salted water to a boil.
Remove the wings from the bugs. Blanch the cicadas in
the boiling water for 1 minute. Transfer the critters to a
bowl of ice water to stop the cooking. Drain the cicadas
and pat dry.
Heat a large wok or sauté pan over high heat. When the
pan begins to smoke, add the oil, remove from the
flame, and add the cicadas.
Return the pan to the heat, add the remaining dry
ingredients, and sauté for about two minutes.
Add the oyster sauce, tamari, and sambal, and sauté
another minute.
Plate and serve immediately. Preferably with carry out
fried rice and an egg roll.

Arroz Verde con Cicadas

Serves 8

Ingredients:

¾ cup + ¼ cup of cilantro
½ cup of parsley
½ cup of epazote (a Mexican herb also known as Jerusalem parsley)
1 clove garlic, diced
½ teaspoon dried oregano leaves
¼ teaspoon cumin
¼ teaspoon cocoa powder
3 cups chicken broth
1 ½ cups white rice
¼ cup oil
2 roasted Poblano chiles, diced
1 Serrano chile (seeded), thinly sliced
½ small white onion, chopped
1 small zucchini, diced
1 cup corn (white or yellow)
1 cup diced carrots
½ cup white wine
1 teaspoon of Kosher salt
3 dozen dry roasted cicadas
1 avocado, diced
1 pound queso fresco, diced

Instructions:

In a blender, mix ¾ cup of cilantro, the parsley, epazote, Serrano chile, garlic, oregano, cumin, cocoa and 1 ½ cups chicken broth until smooth. Heat oil in a large, heavy frying pan over medium heat, add rice.

Arroz Verde con Cicadas – continued

Lightly brown the rice (stir often to prevent sticking). Add Poblano chiles and onion; continue cooking, stirring often, until onions are translucent. Add mixture from blender and continue to cook for about 10min, stirring often. Add zucchini, corn, carrot, and remaining 1 ½ cups broth, white wine and salt; stir well.
As soon as rice comes to a full boil, turn heat to low and cover for 20min. Stir before serving.
Plate and top with cicadas, avocado and queso fresco.

Cicada Pizza

Serves 4

Ingredients:
Dough:

> 1 package active dry yeast (about 2 teaspoons)
> 1 ½ cup warm water (105 to 115°F)
> 1 tablespoon honey
> 2 tablespoons extra-virgin olive oil
> 2 cups all-purpose flour
> 1 teaspoon salt

Topping:

> 8 ounces tomato sauce
> 2 dozen blanched cicadas
> 8 ounces sliced mushrooms, drained
> ½ medium red onion, thinly sliced
> 1/2 cup small to medium arugula leaves
> 1/2 cup grated Parmesan cheese
> 1 to 2 cups shredded Mozzarella cheese

Instructions:

In a stand mixer bowl, dissolve the yeast in the water. Add the honey and stir together. Let sit 2 or 3 minutes or until the water is cloudy. Stir in the olive oil. Combine the flour and salt and add it to the yeast mixture all at once. Mix using the paddle attachment, then change to the dough hook and knead at low speed for 2 minutes. Then turn up to medium speed and knead for about 5 minutes until the dough comes

Cicada Pizza – continued

cleanly away from the sides of the bowl and clusters around the dough hook.

Turn out onto a lightly floured work surface and knead by hand for 2 or 3 minutes longer until the dough is smooth and elastic (not tacky, press it with your finger it should slowly spring back), and it should not feel tacky.

Transfer the dough to a clean, lightly oiled bowl. Cover the bowl tightly with plastic wrap, and leave it in a warm spot to rise for 30 minutes.

Place a pizza stone on the middle rack of the oven and preheat the oven to 500°F.

On a lightly floured surface, stretch (or roll out) the dough to the desired size and thickness (depending on the size pizza you want, you might make two pizzas out of this one batch of dough). Spread tomato sauce onto on dough with the back of spoon. Sprinkle with Parmesan and then Mozzarella. Add mushrooms, onion and cicadas. Transfer the pizzas to the pizza stone and bake 10 to 12 minutes (until the pizza crust is nicely browned).

When pizza is removed from oven, scatter arugula on top, cut into wedges and serve.

Cicada Raisin Oatmeal Cookies
Makes 2 to 3 dozen cookies

Ingredients:

1 cup all-purpose flour

½ teaspoon baking soda

½ teaspoon salt

1 ¼ sticks unsalted butter, softened

½ cup raw/natural sugar (Turbinado)

½ cup packed light brown sugar

1 large egg

½ teaspoon vanilla

½ cup dry roasted cicadas (see page 11), chopped

1 cup raisins

1 ¾ cups old-fashioned rolled oats

Instructions:

Preheat oven to 325°F.

Lightly grease baking sheets (or cover with parchment paper.

In a bowl, stir together oats, flour, baking soda, and salt; set aside.

In a separate bowl, beat together butter, granulated sugar, and brown sugar with an electric mixer until light and airy.

Add egg and vanilla and beat well.

Add oat mixture, cicadas and raisins. Mix until well combined.

Place dough baking sheets in 1 ½ inch balls, 2 inches apart onto.

Bake until golden (about 12 minutes total).

Transfer to racks to cool.

Cicada Crispies

Ingredients:

3 tablespoons butter (or margarine)
4 cups miniature marshmallows
5 cups crisped rice cereal (e.g., Kellogg's Rice Krispies)
1 cup dry roasted cicadas (see page 11), chopped

Instructions:

In large saucepan melt butter over low heat. Add marshmallows and stir until completely melted. Remove from heat.
Add cereal and cicadas. Stir until well coated.
Put mixture into a 13 x 9 x 2-inch pan coated with cooking spray press wax paper evenly on the mixture to make level/even in the pan. Cool. Cut into 2-inch squares. Best if served the same day.

Chocolate Covered Cicadas

Ingredients:

> 1 cup dry roasted cicadas (see page 11)
> 1 cup chocolate chips

Instructions:

Melt the chocolate chips according to packaging (we use a Pyrex measuring cup in the microwave).

Drop in a few cicadas and gently stir to totally cover them in chocolate.

Remove them (we use small fork under the cicada) and place them on wax paper with enough space between them that the chocolate does not touch.

Continue until all the cicadas are covered.

The chocolate will harden overnight (if we are in a hurry we put them in the freezer for about an hour).

Serve when hardened (can be stored in a covered container for a few days).

Sweet Cicada Shish-Kabobs

Serves 5

Courtesy of Zack Lemann, Audubon Butterfly Garden
and Insectarium, New Orleans, LA

Ingredients:
- 20 cicadas
- 1 apple
- Water
- Brown sugar
- Honey
- 4 friends

Instructions:

In a pan, set heat for medium/low and add 4-6 oz. of water (see how soft or crunchy you like the cicadas and use less liquid and more heat if you prefer your bugs somewhat crispy), a tablespoon of brown sugar, and a tablespoon of honey. Stir as it heats. You want to make a thin but sweet liquid. Set the cicadas in the water just to coat them and then place them in a run-in toaster for 10 minutes or so (or use a setting like 175-200 on an oven). While the bugs cook, turn off the heat but keep that liquid! Dice an apple so you have pieces a bit smaller than an individual cicada. When the allotted time has passed, move cicadas back into the pan, add the apples, and cook them on low heat for another 10 minutes. Using a long skewer, spear a cicada and a piece of apple and serve. You can play with the ratio and do 2 bugs per piece of fruit or vice versa depending on what people like. But the point is, everyone will like this!

Cicada Brownies

Ingredients:

¾ cup all-purpose flour
¼ teaspoon baking soda
¾ cup granulated sugar
1 package (12 ounce) semisweet chocolate chips
½ cup dry roasted cicadas (see page 11), cut in half
2 large eggs
1/3 cup butter
2 tablespoons water
1 teaspoon vanilla extract

Instructions:

Preheat oven to 325°. Grease a 9-inch pan.
In a small bowl, mix flour and baking soda.
In a small saucepan combine sugar, butter and water.
Bring to boil over medium heat: remove immediately
from heat.
Stir in 1 cup of chocolate morsels and vanilla until
melted and smooth. Transfer mixture to a medium bowl
and cool completely.
Stir eggs into the cooled chocolate mixture, beating
well. Gradually stir in flour until smooth. Stir remaining
chocolate morsels and nuts into batter. Pour into
greased pan. Bake 30-35 minutes (insert toothpick and
if it comes out clean, brownies are done). Place pan on
rack and cool completely.

Caramel Cicada Crunch

Ingredients:

1 cup brown sugar; packed
½ cup unsalted butter
½ cup corn syrup
4 quarts fresh popped corn
1 cup dry roasted cicadas (see page 11), chopped
½ teaspoon salt
½ teaspoon baking soda
½ teaspoon vanilla extract

Instructions:

Place popcorn in large roasting pan (5 quart) with chopped cicadas and blend together. Set aside. Preheat oven to 250°F. In heavy sauce pan, mix sugar, butter, corn syrup and salt. Stir over medium heat until boiling. Continue to boil, without stirring, for 5 minutes. Remove from heat.
Stir in vanilla, then baking soda (it will foam up). Pour over popped corn and cicadas; mix well to coat.
Place in oven for 1 hour. Stir every 15 minutes while baking. Cool, break apart and serve or store in a tightly sealed container.

ABOUT THE AUTHOR

R. Scott Frothingham is an entrepreneur, consultant, speaker, business coach and author best known for his FastForward Income™ products including *The 15-minute Sales Workout*™. He helps entrepreneurs, managers and sales/marketing executives position themselves for success through skills training and personal development -- along with providing tools for effectively and efficiently training and motivating their teams.

He has written a number of business books including "6-Minute Success Training," "High Conversion E-Mail Copywriting" and "Success-ercize" and the 6-book "Words & Wisdom" series featuring Abraham Lincoln, Mark Twain, Ben Franklin and other iconic Americans.

This is Scott's first cook book.

R. Scott Frothingham

www.ScottFrothingham.com
Facebook: **www.Facebook.com/FastForwardIncome**
Twitter: **@ScottFroth**

Check out this other Cook Book from FastForward Publishing.

Take a look inside ➤

Introduction

A number of years ago I was working for a radio station that was sponsoring a "Barbecue Battle". Once the promotion was over, the winners had been announced and the crowds had gone home, I had the good fortune to sit a spell and jaw with 4 or 5 guys who traveled the barbecue competition circuit. Now these ol' boys ate, drank and slept barbecue. Actually, they drank whiskey and beer, which made for some pretty lively conversation like:

> "I'm hungry; does anybody have any "q" leftover?"

> "Naw, but I gotta couple a steaks I can throw on the grill."

> "Grill? Son, if it ain't smoked, it ain't barbeque!"

> "Just smoked? Boy, get with the program: if it ain't smoked <u>pig</u>, it ain't 'q'!"

> "Damn, Bubba, you couldn't find your ass with both hands and a flashlight! If it ain't A WHOLE PIG in the smoker, it ain't barbecue!"

Well, I just sat back and listened and learned. And drank. And drank some more. And ate some of the best food I'd ever had. And drank some more.

There are some crazy stories (tall tales and true ones) that came out of that night, but those are for other writin's. It's just when I sat down to write this book on barbecue, that night came to mind, so I figured that conversation would be a good place to commence to getting in the mood.

But now that I think about it, I'm almost always in the mood to talk about food, especially barbecue. So, here are some of the recipes we cook in our family. There's a lot of smokin', a bit of grillin', some sides and a dessert. I hope you and your family enjoy makin' and eatin' this food as much as we do.

RECIPES

Cooter Brown's "South Mouth" Books
available at Amazon.com & other retailers

DADDY'S SECRET:
THE BEST DARNED BURGERS EVER

For as long as I can remember, I always liked the burgers my dad cooked on the grill a whole heap more than anybody else's. I wasn't alone. Whenever folks were visitin' and Daddy fired up the grill for burgers, everybody would be askin', "What's your secret for makin' these burgers so good?"

And he'd always answer the same way, "Well the first part is to only flip 'em once. As for the second part, that's for me to know and you to find out."

His reputation as makin' the best burgers in the county hit home one morning at the diner when Miss Bernice leaned across the counter and said, "Cooter, what's it gonna take to get your daddy's burger recipe? I'd serve 'em everyday. Probably double my dinner business."

So, I went home and told him that it was time to pass along the recipe to his favorite son.

> "That's what the publishing folks call a 'teaser'," states Cooter Brown. "Now you gotta buy my book to find out my daddy's secret to making the best darned burgers ever. Of course, can get the cookbook for FREE when you buy my other book *'Cooter Brown's South Mouth: Hillbilly Wisdom, Redneck Observations and Good Ol' Boy Logic'*! Details on page 3, right after the dedication."

Is One of Your Goals to be a Published Author?

We Can Help!

From taking your idea from concept to published book and all steps in between, FastForward Publishing can do it all:

- If your book is already written, we can get it published quickly (Kindle, Nook, paperback edition, etc.).

- If you are already published, we can help you increase sales.

- Even if you just have an idea for a book but don't know how to take the next step, we can help you get your ideas on to paper.

Take the Next Step to Becoming a Published Author:
Contact Us Today

www.FastForwardPublishing.com

Made in the USA
Monee, IL
28 May 2021

69639087R00046